CW00494304

summersdale

JELLYFISH MCSAVELOY

Copyright © Summersdale Publishers Ltd, 2009

Text contributed by David Pearson.

All rights reserved.

No part of this book may be reproduced by any means, nor transmitted, nor translated into a machine language, without the written permission of the publishers.

Condition of Sale
This book is sold subject to the condition that it shall not, by way of trade or otherwise, be lent, re-sold, hired out or otherwise circulated in any form of binding or cover other than that in which it is published and without a similar condition including this condition being imposed on the subsequent publisher.

Summersdale Publishers Ltd
46 West Street
Chichester
West Sussex
PO19 1RP
UK

www.summersdale.com

Printed and bound in Great Britain

ISBN: 978-1-84024-787-9

Substantial discounts on bulk quantities of Summersdale books are available to corporations, professional associations and other organisations. For details telephone Summersdale Publishers on (+44-1243-771107), fax (+44-1243-786300) or email (nicky@summersdale.com).

NUTTY NAMES, SILLY SIGNS AND TONGUE-TWISTING TITLES

HUGH JASS

Contents

Editor's Note

What's in a name? Well, quite a lot, actually. We use our names many times a day, for simple things like introducing ourselves, filling in forms, and, in the case of Harden Long, chatting people up in the pub.

So what happens when a name crops up that is out of the ordinary? There are almost endless reasons for something or someone being given a funny name. Take the case of Treacle Mine Road and Peach Pie Street in Wincanton, Somerset, for example. Sadly, they are not named after the local industries (treacle mining sounds altogether dangerous when you think about it), but instead after roads in the fictional city of Ankh-Morpork from Terry Pratchett's *Discworld* series of novels. A housing developer suggested naming the streets in honour of the books, and someone in the planning department must have been a fan because it was approved.

Other names are more surprising at first glance, as the members of the Idiot Club will know all too well from bitter experience. Although it sounds like an assembly of the lowest-powered minds on the planet, it is actually the official fan club for the band Green Day (it's named after one of their songs). Not that the real explanation will be much good if you drop your membership card in the street for people to see.

Some names are created simply by an error or vagary of translation – or mistranslation, as it were. Such names include Salty Cat, a fruit drink sold across Asia, whose manufacturers probably thought they were giving it a cool, stylish and tempting name.

Then, of course, there are the people who change their name just to stand out from the crowd. This is where the name of this simply wonderful book draws its inspiration – a chap who changed his name from Steven Lane to Jellyfish McSaveloy, just because he enjoyed being different.

This is just a tiny taster of what's to come in the following chapters, which gather together the quirkiest, rarest and most obscure names in one side-splitting volume, guaranteed to make you a) laugh, b) want to read it again and c) change your name to something silly.

So read on to find out who (or what) Minty Clinch is, where you will find a town called Hell, who would be likely to eat Cock Soup and what cummingtonite really is.

Enjoy!

NB: If your name, town or product has made it into this book, congratulations and thank you for making the world a slightly more interesting place.

Your Name is What?

No anthology of funny names would be complete without a list of people whose monikers are a source of amusement wherever they go. Some of the names are accidentally funny, like Alice Pinckass, and then there are those that are just plain weird, like Boliver Shagnasty. Some, obviously bored with their bog-standard names, have changed them by deed poll to something more exotic, while others clearly have very imaginative parents who wanted to give their little darlings a stamp of individuality.

People

This section contains names that appear in telephone directories across the globe – I bet you never considered reading the phone book to be so entertaining…

Terry Bull (male, UK)

Les Plack (male dentist, USA)

Hitler Manila (male, Philippines)

Ray Gunn (male, UK)

Anna Prentice (female, USA)

Joker Arroyo (male, Philippines)

Bill Board (male, USA)

Ray Beams (male, UK)

Dr Leslie Doctor (male, USA)

Rose Bush (female, UK)

Dr Payne (male, USA)

Justin Case (male, UK)

Superman (male, New Zealand)

Teresa Green (female, UK)

Chris Cross (male, UK)

Priti Manek (female, USA)

Urhines Kendall Icy Eight Special K (unknown, USA)
Max Power (male, UK)
Dr Thoulton Surgeon (male, USA)
Mary Christmas (female, UK)
Annette Curtain (female, USA)
Ace Barbers (male, Philippines)
Barb Dwyer (female, UK)
Breece D'J Pancake (male, USA)
Doug Hole (male, UK)
Bumble Ward (male, USA)
Stan Still (male, UK)
Learned Hand (male, USA)
Loser Lane (male, USA)
Tim Burr (male, UK)
Mangled Brown Fence-Post (male, UK)
Ima Hogg (female, USA)
Cardinal Sin (male cardinal, Philippines)
Paige Turner (female, UK)
M3 Sweatt (male, USA)
Helen Back (female, UK)
Jon Blake Cusack 2.0 (male, USA)

Lee King (male, UK)

A B Kovacs (male, USA – his first name is simply the letter 'A')

Adolf Lu Hitler R. Marak (male, India)

Jenny Taylor (female, UK)

Revilo Oliver (male, USA – his name is a palindrome)

Robert Trebor (male actor, USA – his name is also a palindrome)

Anna Sasin (female, UK)

Minty Clinch (female, UK)

Dick Short (male, USA)

Sonny Day (male, UK)

Harry Beavers (male, USA)

Phat Ho (male, USA)

Will Power (male, UK)

Harry Wacker (male, USA)

Jo King (female, UK)

Richard Rubright (male, USA)

Kristie Doubledee (female, USA)

Barry Cade (male, UK)

Arthur Dorkoff (male, USA)

Verbyl Belch (unknown, USA)

Harden Long (male, USA)

Iona Dickey (female, USA)

Carrie Oakey (female, UK)

Drew Peacock (male, UK)

Bolivar Shagnasty (male, USA)

Hazel Nutt (female, UK)

Candy Barr (female, USA)

And finally, we can only hope that the following chap put his name to good use – curing the sick, for example, or at least playing the piano:

Miracle Fingers (male, USA)

Long Names

Feel sorry for these people who must take forever to fill in application forms:

Rodolfo Alfonso Raffaello Piero Filiberto Gugliemli di Valentina d'Antoguella

(This is the full name of film star Rudolph Valentino.)

Siddig El Tahir El Fadil El Siddig El Abderrahman Mohammed Ahmed Abdel Karim El Mahdi

(This Sudanese-born English actor subsequently changed his name to Alexander Siddig to make it easier for his English-speaking fans to pronounce his name.)

Rhodawaktanannacaramellicadayshatunthun-duishimotrincorvetticamelonporchettadawan-tachevrolettaredmondicaphilladelpharazin-naphinneloppiarhoshandiatellyneshiaunn-eveshenk Koyaanisquatsiuth-Darshekkiaka-roqodish Williams

(This Texan girl's name is a combination of words from several languages.)

Louis George Maurice Adolphe Roche Albert Abel Antonio Alexandre Noë Jean Lucien Daniel Eugène Joseph-le-brun Joseph-Barême Thomas Thomas Thomas-Thomas Pierre Arbon Pierre-Maurel Barthélemi Artus Alphonse Bertrand Dieudonné Emanuel Josué Vincent Luc Michel Jules-de-la-plane Jules-Bazin Julio César Jullien

(This French composer's name looks like a 'Best Of' compilation of French boys' names of the 1800s.)

Adolph Blaine Charles David Earl Frederick Gerald Hubert Irvin John Kenneth Lloyd Martin Nero Oliver Paul Quincy Randolph Sherman Thomas Uncas Victor William Xerxes Yancy Zeus Wolfeschlegelsteinhausenbergerdorffvoralternwarengewissenhaftschaferswessenschafewarenwohlgepflegeundsorgfaltigkeitbeschutzenvonangreifendurchihrraubgierigfeindewelchevoralternzwolftausendjahresvorandieerscheinenwandererssteerdemenschderraumschiffgebrauchlichtalsseinursprungvonkraftgestartseinlangefahrthinzwischensternartigraumaufdersuchesodanachdiesternwelchegehabtbewohnbarplanetenkreisedrehensichundwohinderneurassevonverstandigmenschlichkeitkonntefortplanzenundsicherfreuenanlebenslanglichfreudeundruhemitnichteinfurchtvorangreifenvonandererintelligentgeschopfsvonhinzwischensternartigraum Senior

(The ultimate passport filler and the longest registered name in the world, which belongs to a German-born Philadelphian.

One translation of Adolph's surname is as follows:

'Who before ages were conscientious shepherds whose sheep were well tended and diligently protected against attackers who by their rapacity were enemies who 12,000 years ago appeared from the stars to the humans by spaceships with light as an origin of power, started a long voyage within star-like space in search for the star which has habitable planets orbiting and whither the new race of reasonable humanity could thrive and enjoy lifelong happiness and tranquillity without fear of attack from other intelligent creatures from within star-like space.')

This British woman is guaranteed never to forget the alphabet:

Anna Bertha Cecilia Diana Emily Fanny Gertrude Hypatia Inez Jane Kate Louise Maud Nora Ophelia Prudence Quince Rebecca Sarah Teresa Ulysis Venus Winifred Xenophon Yetty Zeus Pepper

Celebrity Offspring

We all know that celebrities live in a different world to the rest of us, but to extend their flights of fantasy to their children by giving them ridiculous names is something else. Here are a few youngsters that are guaranteed to be picked on in the playground…

Kal-El Coppola (son of Nicholas Cage, actor)

Pilot Inspektor (son of Jason Lee, actor)

Fifi Trixibelle, Peaches Honeyblossom and Little Pixie (daughters of Bob Geldof, musician)

Apple (daughter of Chris Martin, musician and Gwyneth Paltrow, actress)

Kyd (son of David Duchovny, actor and Tea Leoni, actress)

Sage Moonblood (son of Sylvester Stallone, actor)

Destry (daughter of Steven Spielberg, film director)

Everly Bear (son of Anthony Keidis, musician)

Kevlar (son of Kimbo Slice, martial arts fighter)

Moxie Crimefighter and Zolten Penn (daughter and son of Penn Killette, comedian)

God (daughter of Grace Slick, musician)

Bluebell Madonna (daughter of Geri Halliwell, singer)

Jermajesty (son of Jermaine Jackson, musician)

Ocean, Sonnet and True (children of Forest Whittaker, actor)

Rocket, Racer, Rebel and Rogue (children of Robert Rodriguez, actor)

Peanut Kai (son of Ingo Rademacher, actor)

Poesy Emmeline Fibonacci Nautilus Taylor (daughter of Cory Doctorow, journalist and Alice Taylor, TV editor)

Tu Morrow (daughter of Rob Morrow, actor and Debbon Ayer, actress)

Here's a man who seems to have given his children the silliest names he could think of, but justified it by explaining that their first names wouldn't define them anywhere near as much as their surname:

Moon Unit, Dweezil and Diva Muffin

(children of Frank Zappa, musician)

Deed Poll

How far would you go to mark yourself out from the crowd? These wacky characters went further than most and for some surprising reasons…

General Ninja Ant

(This man from Essex, UK, was a victim of bullying and believed this new name would help deter his enemies.)

Jellyfish McSaveloy

(This British man changed his name from Steven Lane – just for fun.)

Yahoo Serious

(This Australian actor changed his name and tried to sue 'Yahoo!' the Internet search engine for trademark infringement – he lost.)

Saxon Knight

(This woman from Devon, UK, changed her name from Janice Glover to display her patriotism.)

Aron Mufasa Columbo Fonzerelli Ball In A Cup Boogie Woogie Brown

(This man from Derby, UK, altered his name in reference to his hobbies.)

Trout Fishing in America

(This man from California, USA, changed his name to show his appreciation of the novella of the same name, written by Richard Brautigan.)

N'Tom The Haymaker Haywardyou-liketocomebacktomine

(This man doesn't remember changing his name, due to being drunk when it happened, but is pleased with it nonetheless.)

Happy Adjustable Spanners

(This person also changed his name whilst drunk, but is less sure about his new title.)

Mc Lovin

(This man named himself after a character in the film *Superbad*.)

Captain Fantastic Faster Than Superman Spiderman Batman Wolverine Hulk And The Flash Combined

(This man changed his name to be unique – which appears to have worked.)

Austin Haddock

(This British politician changed his name to show support for his fishermen constituents who were being affected by a haddock-fishing ban.)

Byron (Low Tax) Looper

(This American politician changed his name to garner support for his election campaign.)

Miss Alice

(This male New Zealand lawyer changed his name to make a stand against the way the New Zealand legal system was run from the inside.)

Nigel Freemarajuana

(This Australian politician fought for the legalisation of cannabis and changed his name to reflect his views.)

Captain Beany

(This man simply renamed himself after his favourite food.)

DotComGuy

(This man changed his name as part of a publicity stunt in which he remained inside his house for a whole year, using the Internet to supply himself with essentials and entertainment.)

GoldenPalace.com

(This woman auctioned her name as advertising space and netted $15,000 from Golden Palace Casino for her trouble.)

Zachary Zzzzzzzzzra

(This man changed his name so that people could find him more easily in the phone directory.)

Kamakazi

(This BMX racer changed his name to reflect the nature of his sport.)

Chad Ochocinco

(This American football player changed his name so that it would read 'eight five' in Spanish – 85 being his playing number during games.)

Nigel Bottomface

(This British man changed his name for a £50 pound bet.)

Manchestar Yunayted

(This man from the Bulgarian town of Svishtov renamed himself after his favourite football team.)

John Portsmouth Football Club Westwood

(This man, another football fanatic, named himself after the club he has supported since childhood.)

Here's a ray of light at the end of the ridiculous name tunnel: the New Zealand girl on whom this unfortunate name was bestowed was allowed to legally change it at the age of only nine due to being (unsurprisingly) bullied at school:

Talula Does The Hula From Hawaii

The Cream of the Cornish

You might think it indulgent to have a section from a single county in the UK, but the following names taken from the Cornwall Record Office's birth register – dating back to the sixteenth century – prove that Cornwall is just that little bit special. Some of them probably weren't so funny when they were bestowed on children in days gone by, but that shouldn't stop us from taking the opportunity to look back and show our mirthful appreciation retrospectively…

Truth Bullock

Fanny Job

Weymouth Lancaster

Judah Bunny

Minnie Daffodil Treverrow

Obedience Ginger

Sophia Cheese

Honour Fraud

Charity Chilly

Gentle Fudge

Unite Bunny

Flower Garland
Philadelphia Bunnyface
Silence Green
Cowbridge Jago
Elizabeth Disco
Freke Dorothy Fluck Lane
Marmaduke Jewel
Dinah Laundry
Ffaithfull Ffillips
Longrocanger Long
Pretty Pinkey
Mahershalalhashbaz Richards
Mary Mutton
Flower Champion
Garthered Trebarfoot
Epiphany Lullaby
Clobery Silly
Offspring Gurney
Patience Creep
Posthumos Dadson
Fanny Forward

Orange Libbye
Admonition Danger
Prudence Rentfree
Edward Evil
Patience Muck
Talent Ferret
Elizabeth Pee
Blodwen Gripe
Alice Pinckass
Weary Jackett
Kitty Jealous
Faithful Nettle
Foscurinus Turtluff Dyer
Friday Screetch
Hapless Pellowe
Discipline Richards
Gilbert Thick
Epiphany Wills
Patience Upright
Prissy Willmet
Fanny Scum

Lulilia Crap
Thomas Shewvalbottem
Cornelius Kidney
Hephzibah Lillycrap
Phillipa Offal
Admonition Mould
Florinda Organ
Peter Piddle
Narcissus Backway
Freak Ustick
Philidelphia Poope
Maudlin Mundy
Pee Rodda
Thomas Tynckler
Lower Polpednick
Clement Rude
Richard Wyndyeate
Noah Flood
Defiance Penfold
Absolom Beaglehole
Fanny Cobbledick

Elizabeth Poo
Sufferance Millet
Faithful Cock
Jeedy Polestag
Loveday Rutter

You would expect this name to have belonged to the naughtiest girl in class:

Fanny Moody Manners

People Named After Other Things

Plenty of people are passionate about something in their life, whether it be rock climbing, jazz music or, er, trainspotting. You might even be fanatical about your own interests, but are you fervent enough to be named after your hobby – or your parents' hobby? Well, it seems that some people are…

James Dr No From Russia with Love Goldfinger Thunderball You Only Live Twice On Her Majesty's Secret Service Diamonds Are Forever Live and Let Die The Man with the Golden Gun The Spy Who Loved Me Moonraker For Your Eyes Only Octopussy A View to a Kill The Living Daylights Licence to Kill GoldenEye Tomorrow Never Dies The World Is Not Enough Die Another Day Casino Royale Bond

(David Fearn from Walsall, UK, changed his name to the titles of every James Bond movie at the time in order to celebrate the release of the latest Bond film.)

Anthony Philip David Terry Frank Donald Stanley Gerry Gordon Stephen James Oatway

(An English footballer named after all 11 players of a Queens Park Rangers Football Club side.)

Creedence Clearwater Couto

(A Brazilian football player named after his parents' favourite rock and blues band.)

Armand Hammer

(An American industrialist named after the 'Arm and Hammer' that represented the Socialist Labor Party.)

Metallica Tomaro

(A man named after the heavy metal band.)

Optimus Prime

(This American reserve soldier changed his name to a character from the popular cartoon series *Transformers*.)

Tarquin Fin-tim-lin-bin-whin-bim-lim-bus-stop-F'tang-F'tang-Olé-Biscuitbarrel

(This man was born John Desmond Lewis but changed his name when he stood as a member of the Monster Raving Loony Party in the 1981 Crosby by-election, UK. The name stems from a character of the same name on the television programme *Monty Python's Flying Circus*, in which the character wins the Luton by-election.)

Donald Duck

(This person was named after the legendary Walt Disney cartoon character.)

Cajus Julius Caesar

(This man is a member of the German parliament.)

Zeppelin Wai Wong

(This person was named after the Graf Zeppelin airship, which flew over his place of birth and inspired his parents' choice.)

Naming your child after the place of conception is not uncommon, hence Brooklyn Beckham, but in this case the parents have perhaps taken the idea too far:

Number 16 Bus Shelter

Cheese Problems Solved and Other Serious Reading Matter

They say you should never judge a book by its cover and this seems pertinent advice judging by this next selection of titles. But it is also within the pages of seemingly unobtrusive tomes that the most bizarre character names serve to trip you up each time you encounter them. And it is not just book titles that make you do a double take, but a trip to the corner shop and a browse of the magazines with titles such as *A Bear's Life* and *Miniature Donkey Talk* can also prove more enlightening or diverting than you first thought.

Books

Some books are clearly named with a twinkle in the eye and a keenly developed sense of irony, while others have obviously been given silly names entirely by accident. It's up to you to decipher which is which…

Jehovah's Witness Protection Program

Kelley, Rich (2008, Western Star Publishing)

Why Cucumbers Are Better Than Men

The Cucumber Group (1983, M. Evans and Company)

The Moose Cookbook: Over 100 Ways to Cook Your Moose

Koneazny, Jack (1997, General Store Publishing House)

Embracing Your Big Fat Ass: An Owner's Manual

Banks, Laura, and Barber, Janette and O'Donnell, Rosie (2008, Atria)

Slow Fat Triathlete: Live Your Athletic Dreams in the Body You Have Now

Williams, Jayne, and Anderson, Tim (2004, Da Capo Press)

Sharks That Walk On Land

Palmer, Ron (2006, Trafford Publishing)

West Country Silver Spoons and Their Makers

Kent, Timothy Arthur (1992, J. H. Bourdon-Smith)

You're an Idiot, and People Talk About You Behind Your Back!

Onetowne, Alastair (2006, Dog Ear Publishing)

The Hollow Chocolate Bunnies of the Apocalypse

Rankin, Robert (2003, Gollancz)

Soup: A Way of Life

Kafka, Barbara (1998, Artisan)

Life in a Bucket of Soil
Silverstein, Alvin, and Silverstein, Virginia (2000, Dover Publications)

Growing Older With Your Teeth or Something Like Them
Keith, D. D. S., and Robinson, A. (1998, Synergy Publishers)

Castration: The Advantages and the Disadvantages
Cheney, Victor T. (2003, AuthorHouse)

Excrement in the Late Middle Ages: Sacred Filth and Chaucer's Fecopoetics
Signe Morrison, Susan (2008, Palgrave Macmillan)

Cooking with Pooh: Yummy Tummy Cookie Cutter Treats
(1995, Mouse Works)

Anybody Can be Cool… But Awesome Takes Practice

Peterson, Lorraine (1988, Bethany House Publishers)

How to Talk about Books You Haven't Read

Bayard, Pierre (2007, Bloomsbury USA)

Are Women Human?: And Other International Dialogues

MacKinnon, Catharine A. (2006, Belknap Press of Harvard University Press)

Foreskin's Lament: A Memoir

Auslander, Shalom (2007, Riverhead Hardcover)

Curbside Consultation of the Colon: 49 Clinical Questions

Cash, Brookes D. (2008, Slack)

Don't Tell Mom I Work on the Rigs: She Thinks I'm a Piano Player in a Whorehouse

Carter, Paul (2007, Da Capo Press)

Who Cares about Elderly People?

Adams, Pam (1990, Child's Play International)

What's Your Poo Telling You?

Sheth, Anish, and Richman, Josh (2007, Chronicle Books)

Cunt Colouring Book

Corinne, Tee (1989, Last Gasp)

How to Good-bye Depression: If You Constrict Anus 100 Times Everyday. Malarkey? Or Effective Way?

Nishigaki, Hiroyuki (2000, iUniverse)

Zen of Farting

Gud Wan, Reepah (2003, Frog Books)

Old Tractors and the Men Who Love Them: How to Keep Your Tractors Happy and Your Family Running

Welsch, Roger (1995, MBI)

The Stray Shopping Carts of Eastern North America: A Guide to Field Identification

Montague, Julian (2006, Abrams Image)

Teddy Bear Cannibal Massacre

Lieder, Tim W. (2005, Dybbuk Press)

The Big Book of Lesbian Horse Stories

Surkis, Alisa, and Nolan, Monica (2002, Kensington)

People Who Don't Know They're Dead: How They Attach Themselves to Unsuspecting Bystanders and What to Do About It

Hill, Gary Leon (2005, Weiser Books)

How to Shit in the Woods: An Environmentally Sound Approach to a Lost Art

Meyer, Kathleen (2004, Ten Speed Press)

How to Avoid Huge Ships

Trimmer, John W. (1993, Cornell Maritime Press)

Whose Bottom is This?

Lynch, Wayne (2000, Walrus Books)

The History of Lesbian Hair

Dugger, Mary (1996, Main Street Books)

Bombproof Your Horse: Teach Your Horse to be Confident, Obedient, and Safe, No Matter What You Encounter

Pelicano, Rick, and Tjaden, Lauren (2004, Trafalgar Square Books)

Reusing Old Graves: A Report on Popular British Attitudes

Davies, Douglas, and Shaw, Alastair (1995, Shaw & Sons)

How to Write a How to Write Book

Piddock, Brian, and Connolly, Anthony (2007, Neil Rhodes Books)

I Was Tortured by the Pygmy Love Queen

McCutcheon, Jasper (2007, Nazca Plains)

Cheese Problems Solved

McSweeney, P. L. H. (2007, Woodhead Publishing)

Circumcisions by Appointment: Life in Eighteenth Century Manchester

Westall, Roy (1999, Reword Publishers)

The Line of Cleavage under Elizabeth

Birt, Henry Norbert (1909, Catholic Truth Society)

Queer Shipmates

Campbell, Archibald Bruce (1962, Phoenix House)

Old Dykes I Have Known

Charnley, P. R. (1996, Barny Books)

Penetrating Wagner's Ring: An Anthology

Digaetani, John Louis (1991, Da Capo)

Knots for Everyone: With Whippings and Lashings

(2001, Guide Association)

Boobs: As Seen by John Henry

Vere Hobart, George (2009, BiblioLife)

Dangerous Drugs: An Easy-to-use Reference for Parents and Professionals

Falkowsi, Carol (2003, Hazelden)

Fish Who Cried Wolf

Donaldson, Julia (2008, Arthur A. Levine Books)

How to Draw a Straight Line: A Lecture on Linkages

Kempe, Alfred Bray (1877, Cornell University Library)

Phone Calls from the Dead

Brenner, Wendy (2001, Algonquin Books of Chapel Hill)

Premature Burial and How It May be Prevented: With Special Reference to Trance, Catalepsy, and Other Forms of Suspended Animation

Tebb, William, and Vollum, Edward Perry (1896, Swann Sonnenschein & Co)

Gunrunning for Fun and Profit

Benson, Ragnar (1986, Paladin)

Life as I Have Known it Has Been Finger Lickin' Good

Sanders, Harland (1974, Creation House)

Divorces and Names Changed in Maryland by Act of the Legislature, 1634-1867

Meyer, Mary K. (2007, Heritage Books)

How to Pose with a Fish

Achterhof, Carole (2000, Bare Bones Books)

Is There Sex After Death?

Abel, Alan, and Abel, Jeanne (1976, Bantam Books)

The Romance of Cement

Edison Portland Cement Company (1926, Livermore & Knight)

Shipping Semen? How to Have a Successful Experience

Ahmed, Pennie (1998, Winlock Publishing Company)

Nuclear War: What's in it for You?

Ground Zero War Foundation (1982, Pocket Books)

The Fangs of Suet Pudding

Adams Farr (1944, Gerald G. Swan)

The New Well-Tempered Sentence: A Punctuation Handbook for the Innocent, the Eager, and the Doomed

Gordon, Karen Elizabeth (2003, Mariner Books)

Living with Crazy Buttocks

Cooke, Kaz (2001, Penguin)

Italian Without Words

Cangelosi, Don, and Delli Carpini, Joseph (2008, Summersdale)

One would imagine that this book contains practical advice for anyone who needs to get somewhere in a hurry, but is lacking the means to do so:

How to Steal a Car

Hautman, Pete (2009, Scholastic Press)

Fictional Characters

Script and literary authors have an unlimited artistic licence. It's often children's authors such as Roald Dahl who boast the most fantastical character names in their stories, but occasionally the more sedate book or film unexpectedly wheels out a peach of a name…

Milo Minderbinder

Catch 22 – Joseph Heller

Phaethon Prime Rhadamanth Humodified (augment) Uncomposed, Indepconciousness, Base Neuroformed, Silver-Gray Manorial Schola, Era 7043 (the 'Reawakening')

The Golden Age – John C. Wright

Mustapha Mond

Brave New World – Aldous Huxley

Major Major Major Major

Catch 22 – Joseph Heller

Slartibartfast

The Hitchhiker's Guide to the Galaxy – Douglas Adams

Hiro Protagonist

Snow Crash – Neal Stephenson

Cut Me Own Throat Dibbler

The *Discworld* novels – Terry Pratchett

Seldom Seen Smith

The Monkey Wrench Gang – Edward Abbey

Dr Michael Hfuhruhurr

The Man with Two Brains (1983)

General Jack D. Ripper

Dr. Strangelove or: How I Learned to Stop Worrying and Love the Bomb (1964)

J. Cheever Loophole

At the Circus (1939)

Alexander Throttlebottom

Of Thee I Sing (1972)

Filthy McNasty
The Bank Dick (1940)

Biggus Dickus
Life of Brian (1979)

Kissy Suzuki
You Only Live Twice (1967)

Alotta Fagina
Austin Powers: International Man of Mystery (1997)

If only everyone would take a leaf out of *Monty Python*'s book when it comes to pronouncing difficult names:

Raymond Luxury Yacht (pronounced 'Throatwobbler Mangrove')
Monty Python's Flying Circus (1969)

Charles Dickens' Characters

With his novels containing a combination of gritty realism and flights of fantasy, some of the character names in Charles Dickens' stories certainly lighten the tone of his sometimes bleak storylines. Here is a list of the best of them…

Mr Bumble *(Oliver Twist)*

Ebenezer Scrooge *(A Christmas Carol)*

Mr Gradgrind *(Hard Times)*

Wopsle *(Great Expectations)*

Mr Micawber *(David Copperfield)*

Wackford Squeers *(Nicholas Nickleby)*

Mr Muddlebranes *(Mudfog and Other Sketches)*

Polly Toodle *(Dombey and Son)*

Mr Pecksniff *(Martin Chuzzlewit)*

Mr Podsnap *(Our Mutual Friend)*

Luke Honeythunder *(The Mystery of Edwin Drood)*

Mr Pumblechook *(Great Expectations)*

Professor Pumpinskull *(Mudfog and Other Sketches)*

Mr Sweedlepipe *(Martin Chuzzlewit)*

Uriah Heep *(David Copperfield)*

Considering Dickens' social activism, some of the names he chose for the poverty-stricken and orphaned characters were less than sympathetic:

Sloppy *(Our Mutual Friend)*

P. G. Wodehouse's Characters

Wodehouse's silly names don't leap out at you but sneak up on you unawares. Enjoy this short list, which includes some of his best (and most inventive) character names...

Honoria Glossop *(Jeeves and the Greasy Bird)*

Zenobia Hopwood *(Joy in the Morning)*

Bingo Little *(Jeeves in the Springtime)*

Gussie Fink-Nottle *(Right-Ho, Jeeves)*

Lady Julia Fish *(Blandings Castle* series)

Barmy Fotheringay-Phipps *(Barmy in Wonderland)*

Stilton Cheesewright *(Jeeves and the Feudal Spirit)*

Lady Cynthia Wickhammersley *(The Inimitable Jeeves)*

Lady Hermione Wedge *(Blandings Castle* series)

Clarence MacAndrew Chugwater *(The Swoop!: Or How Clarence Saved England)*

And finally, making superb use of the vagaries of the illogical silent 'p' seen so often across the English language:

Rupert Psmith *(Leave it to Psmith)*

Magazine Titles

Sometimes you can develop an interest in quite an unusual hobby – but luckily there seems to be a magazine to meet everyone's needs...

Girls and Corpses

(This magazine gives the best advice on how to get the most out of your girls and corpses – how to arrange them for photo shoots and hotspots to visit together.)

Miniature Donkey Talk

(A magazine for miniature donkey owners and enthusiasts – the 'talk' in the title refers to the discussion of the animals, not the banter between the donkeys themselves, sadly.)

Modern Drunkard

('Standing up for your right to get falling down drunk since 1996', this magazine contains articles on getting drunk, falling over and reading about it.)

A Bear's Life

(A lifestyle magazine for hairy male homosexuals and their admirers – honestly, it is.)

And for all those super-fans of farm animals out there:

Sheep!

Is This the Way to Balls Cross?

Now for the big one, the section you've all been waiting for (or, if you live in Shitterton in Dorset, the part you have been dreading).

UK

Who was it that thought to give a beauty spot in Worcestershire the name Lickey End? Perhaps Balls Green was named after an unfortunate medical affliction? And what about the rather unsavoury Spital in the Street in Lincolnshire? It is amazing what passes the censors – some are quite whimsical, like the village of Bunny in Nottinghamshire, while others, like Wetwang for instance, are just plain rude...

Worlds End (Berkshire)

Lower Dicker (East Sussex)

Claxby Pluckacre (Lincolnshire)

Balls Cross (West Sussex)

Booze (North Yorkshire)

Willy Knot (Pembrokeshire)

Nether Poppleton (North Yorkshire)

Cold Christmas (Hertfordshire)

Yelling (Cambridgeshire)

Cocking (West Sussex)

Middle Wallop (Hampshire)

Fattahead (Aberdeenshire)

Wetwang (Yorkshire)

East Breast (Western Scotland)

Yonder Bognie (Aberdeenshire)

New Invention (Shropshire)

North Piddle (Worcestershire)

Jump (South Yorkshire)

Crackpot (North Yorkshire)

Great Cockup (Cumbria)

Maudlin (West Sussex)

Penisarwaen (Clwyd)

Crapstone (Devon)

Staines (Middlesex)

Thong (Kent)

Penistone (South Yorkshire)

Twatt (Orkney)

Shitterton (Dorset)

Lord Hereford's Knob (Powys)

Bonkle (Lanarkshire)

Bunny (Nottinghamshire)

Stocking (Herefordshire)

Nut Crackers (Devon)

One would hope that the residents of this village haven't been cursed by the name of their home:

Ugley (Essex)

It apparently means 'woodland clearing of a man named Ugga'. And take a moment to feel some sympathy for the unfortunate members of the Ugley Women's Institute, who after repeated jibes were forced to rename themselves with the more pedestrian Women's Institute of Ugley.

USA

Picture, if you will, a group of settlers still damp and stiff from their long journey across the ocean from England to America. They begin to give names to the places they see around them. One has come from Norfolk, so he suggests naming a town after his home county. Fair enough. How about calling this place Plymouth, another suggests, after the place we sailed from. No problem, they all say. Suddenly, a quiet man at the back pipes up. Why not, he offers, name the next town along Knob Lick? No one ever looks at him in the same way again.

This story may or may not have happened, but the point is you have to question what on earth the first settlers were thinking when they came up with the following names…

Phallus (Utah)

Dead Horse (Creek Alaska)

Archie (Louisiana)

Knob Lick (Missouri)

Lorida (Florida)

Bacon (Indiana)

Hippo (Kentucky)

Ben Franklin (Texas)

Hot Coffee (Mississippi)

Truth or Consequences (New Mexico)
Gayville (South Dakota)
Ben Hur (Texas)
Accident (Maryland)
Looneyville (Ohio)
Bland (Virginia)
What Cheer (Iowa)
Two Egg (Florida)
King Arthur's Court (Michigan)
Sweet Lips (Tennessee)
Bong Recreation Area (Wisconsin)
Peculiar (Missouri)
Chugwater (Wyoming)
Happy Camp (California)
Eek (Alaska)
George (Washington)
Papa (Hawaii)
Dinkytown (Minnesota)
Greasy Corner (Arkansas)
Intercourse (Pennsylvania)
Frankenstein (Missouri)

Bald Knob (Arkansas)
Knockemstiff (Ohio)
Between (Georgia)
Napoleon (North Dakota)
Uncertain (Texas)
Rabbit Hash (Kentucky)
Buddha (Indiana)
Shoofly (North Carolina)
Big Foot (Texas)
Cheesequake (New Jersey)
Spread Eagle (Wisconsin)
Tightwad (Missouri)
Pocahontas (Arkansas)
Bingo (Maine)
Wynot (Nebraska)
Romeo (Michigan)
Wimp (California)
Frostproof (Florida)
Oblong (Illinois)
Looneyville (Texas)
Ruff Starbuck (Washington)

Diagonal (Iowa)
Plain Dealing (Los Angeles)
Wahoo (Nebraska)
Beans Corner (Maine)
Disappointment (Kentucky)
Useful (Missouri)
Bath Addition (Pennsylvania)
Ho-Ho-Kus (New Jersey)
Satan's Kingdom (Vermont)
Imalone (Wisconsin)
Pahrump (Nevada)
Horneytown (North Carolina)
Odd (West Virginia)
Tarzan (Texas)
Hicksville (New York)
Okay (Arkansas)
Drain (Oregon)
Uncle Sam (Louisiana)
Loyalsockville (Pennsylvania)
Red Shirt (South Dakota)
Bumpass Hell (California)

Nameless (Tennessee)

Static (Kentucky)

Twitty (Texas)

Eureka (Nevada)

Goochland (Virginia)

Ubet (Wisconsin)

Zap (North Dakota)

Whiskey Dick Mountain (Washington State)

Santa Claus (Georgia)

Flasher (North Dakota)

Monkeys Eyebrow (Kentucky)

Slaughterville (Oklahoma)

And finally, imagine going here to retire:

Bitter End (Tennessee)

Australia

Imagine having this conversation anywhere but Australia:

'G'day, mate. Don't see you very often in Nowhere Else. Is that a new pickup?'

'Yeah, mate. I just bought it from the dealer up at Iron Knob.'

'Ah, right. You coming down to Cocklebiddy next Tuesday for the cattle drive?'

'Nah, mate – I've got an appointment up at the next town that day.'

'Watanobbi?'

'Yeah, that's it, mate.'

Mooball (New South Wales)

Cocklebiddy (Western Australia)

Hat Head (New South Wales)

Iron Knob (South Australia)

Burrumbuttock (New South Wales)

Jimboomba (Queensland)

Nevertire (New South Wales)

Nowhere Else (Tasmania)

Diehard (New South Wales)

Chinamans Knob (Victoria)

Poowong (New South Wales)
Watanobbi (New South Wales)
Wonglepong (Queensland)
Finger Post (New South Wales)

Now for a place whose name is guaranteed to make you feel hungry every time you visit – and whose cafes must be doing a roaring trade in all-day breakfasts:

Eggs and Bacon Bay (Tasmania)

Rest of World

And if you need some inspiration for your next holiday destination…

Cascade d'Arse (France)

Fucking (Austria)

Dildo (Finland)

Batman (Turkey)

Arsoli (Italy)

Come By Chance (Canada)

Herpes (France)

Boring (Denmark)

Titz (Germany)

Whakapapa (New Zealand – in Maori, 'wh' is pronounced as the English 'f')

Druid (Canada)

Moron (Spain)

Muff (Ireland)

Condom (France)

Windpassing (Austria)

Ebenezer (Canada)

Boom (Belgium)

Poo (Spain)

Fuchū (Japan)

Mermaid (Canada)

Pukë (Albania)

Brest (France)

Lake Minnewanka (Canada)

Hell (Norway)

Binges (France)

Spital (Austria)

Mozart (Canada)

Petting (Germany)

Bendova (Czech Republic)

Dong (Germany)

Bra (Italy)

Cupids (Canada)

Middelfart (Denmark)

Puke (Albania)

Búger (Spain)

Seymen (Turkey)

Monster (The Netherlands)

Vulcan (Canada)

Bastardo (Italy)

Sexmoan (Philippines)

Le Tampon (Reunion)

Asbestos (Canada)

Tosa (Japan)

Wank (Germany)

Xena (Canada)

Cum (Ireland)

Swastika (Canada)

Here's the worst, followed by the ultimate, address for all men out there:

Little Dix (Anguilla)

Longdong (China)

Long Place Names

Here are a few place names that are guaranteed to make you tongue-tied when asking for directions:

Llanfairpwllgwyngyllgogerychwyrndrobwlll-lantysiliogogogoch

(A Welsh town which means, 'The church of St Mary in the hollow of white hazel trees near the rapid whirlpool by St Tysilio's of the red cave.')

Tetaumatawhakatangihangakoauaotamateau-rehaeaturipukapihimaungahoronukupokai-whenuaakitanarahu

(A hill situated near Porangahau, in New Zealand.)

Krungthepmahanakornamornratanakosin-mahintarayutthayamahadilokphopnopparat-rajathaniburiromudomrajaniwesmahasathar-namornphimarnavatarnsathitsakkattiyavi-sanukamprasit

(The official Thai name for what we know as Bangkok.)

The place name that comes in at probably the fourth longest in the world is Los Angeles, or at least its original full name:

El Pueblo de Nuestra Senora la Reina de los Angeles de Porciúncula

Street Names

Just imagine for a moment living in a street with one of these names. OK, you would probably enjoy being able to tell people casually in the pub that you live in Psycho Path, but imagine the embarrassment of informing people in a busy post office that you live in Mincing Lane or Wanker's Corner...

Psycho Path (Michigan, USA)
Mincing Lane (London, UK)
Wanker's Corner (Oregon, USA)
Butthole Lane (Leicestershire, UK)
Juggs Road (East Sussex, UK)
Bell End (West Midlands, UK)
Spooky Hollow (North Carolina, USA)
Butts Wynd (Edinburgh, UK)
Crotch Crescent (Oxfordshire, UK)
Tumbledown Dick Road (Oxfordshire, UK)
Peach Pie Street (Somerset, UK)
Titty Ho (Northamptonshire, UK)
Peepee Falls Street (Hawaii, USA)
Cockshut Road (East Sussex, UK)

Slutshole Lane (Norfolk, UK)
Pill Jerk Road (Tennessee, USA)
Rampant Horse Street (Norfolk, UK)
Poopoo Place (Hawaii, USA)
Treacle Mine Road (Somerset, UK)
No Name (New Mexico, USA)
Friendly (North Carolina, USA)
Salubrious Passage (Swansea, UK)

Here's a street in which it's best not to go wandering after dark lest you step in something you wish you hadn't:

Dirty Ankle Road (North Carolina, USA)

Branded

The misguided thought processes and often bad translation of foreign brand names is a classic example of accidental humour, and in what can be the most surprising of places. Here are some great instances of keen product branding that have flopped horribly in the process of translation.

Asia

Coolpis (drink)

Water Salad (soft drink)

Diet Water (water brand)

Final Fantasy Potion (soft drink)

God (canned coffee)

Pet Sweat (dog sports drink)

Deeppresso (coffee)

PROFiT ('body profitable water')

Wild Drip (coffee)

My Juice (orange juice)

Salty Cat (canned fruit juice)

Monkey Fizz (canned fruit juice)

2% Human Water (water)

Biggy (drink)

Creap (powdered dairy creamer)

Pet Glass (barley grass for cats)

Casual Style Hump (bag)

Painapple Candy (sweet)

Cock Banana in Syrup (tinned fruit)

Asse (chocolate sweet)
Almond Big Bar: Mini (chocolate bar)
Eye Powder (blueberry tablet)
Men's Pocky Chocolate (chocolate snacks)
Coming (lemon-flavoured sweet)
Mother Stick (chocolate biscuit sticks)
Jesus Body (soap)
Pocari Sweat (health drink)
Men's Spray: Super Hard (hairspray)
Perfect Eye Remover (eye make-up remover)
Life Yell (tissues)
Mommy Hot (baby wipes)
Happy Whip (foaming sponge)
Nail Remover (nail polish remover)
Gross Air (hairspray)
HairLess Milk (hair remover)
Olfactory Air Freshener: Pussy (cat-scented air freshener)
Pity (toilet paper)
LSD (training potty)
Badiet (diet pills)

Homo Soap (soap)
Animal Colon (air freshener)
Goon (nappies)
Disposable Moose Traps (mousetraps)

This product may make you think twice before reaching across your desk to put your hand on it:

Sperm (computer mouse)

Rest of World

Bum Bum Banane (ice cream, Germany)

Shito Mix (mixed pepper, Ghana)

Big Nuts (chocolate, Belgium)

Jussipussi (bread, Finland)

Anis (aniseed, Sweden)

Erektus (energy drink, Romania)

Mini-Dickmann's (chocolate, Germany)

Fart (health drink, Poland)

Shitto (pepper sauce, Ghana)

Cock Soup (soup, Jamaica)

Poo Tofu (tofu, Indonesia)

Slowpokes (chocolates, Canada)

Kräpp (toilet paper, Sweden)

Fat Pig (chocolate, USA)

Tender Nuts (chocolate bar, Slovakia)

Smack (instant noodles, Hungary)

Bonka (coffee, Spain)

Fuca (laxative, France)

Homo Milk (milk, USA)

Snögg (dog food, Norway)
Ars (rat poison, Saudi Arabia)
Golden Gaytime (ice cream, Australia)
Vergina (lager, Greece)
Pee Cola (soft drink, Ghana)
Ayds (diet sweets, USA)
Wack Off! (insect repellent, Australia)
SARS (soft drink, New Zealand)
666 (cold medicine, USA)
Choky Choc (breakfast cereal, Portugal)
Chilly (feminine hygiene soap, Italy)
Mukki Milk (milk, Finland)
Happy End (toilet paper, Germany)

And finally, never has the phrase 'not to be used internally' been so relevant to a product as this:

Colon (washing powder, Spain)

Vehicle Names

Car companies are renowned for extravagant advertising gimmicks and over-the-top product launches, but even the most over-optimistic marketing guru would surely spot the immediate problem with these car names…

Detroit Fish (Tang Hua)
Mini Active Urban Sandal (Mitsubishi)
Homy Super Long (Nissan)
Dictator (Studebaker)
Rural Nanny (Geely PU)
Autozam Carol MeLady (Mazda)
Probe (Ford)
Scrum Wagon (Mazda)
Estima Lucida G Luxury Joyful Canopy (Toyota)
Sambar Dias Astonish!! (Subaru)
Big Thumb Harmonised Truck (Nissan)
Every Joy Pop Turbo (Suzuki)
Bongo Friendee (Mazda)
Country Squire (Ford)
Big Horn (Isuzu)

Mum 500 Shall We Join Us (Mitsubishi)
Rugged Field Sports Resin Top (Daihatsu)
Life Dunk (Honda)
Mysterious Utility Wizard (Isuzu)
Canter Guts (Mitsubishi)
Cedric (Nissan)
Proceed Marvie Will Breeze (Mazda)
Domingo Aladdin (Subaru)
Bongo Brawny (Mazda)
Alto Afternoon Tea (Suzuki)
Pantryboy Supreme (Yamaha)

Here's one product that's so good they named it twice:

Van Van (Suzuki)

Except it's a motorbike…

Bad Company

What better way to stick in the memory of customers and potential trade than with a catchy name? But it is when browsing for a website for something as innocent as Italian electrical services company Powergen Italia that the likelihood of stumbling on something completely inappropriate becomes unavoidable. And woe betide anyone searching for the Pen Island website.

Business Names

You may want a catchy name when starting up a company, but consider how others might perceive it; if you name your travel agency 'Go Away', there's a good chance that people might do just that – and we don't mean on one of your holidays…

Mammoth Erection (scaffolders, Canada)

Big Ass Fans (fan manufacturer, USA)

Air Head (waterless toilet company, USA)

Go Away (travel agent, USA)

Shamrock Diamonds (jewellers, USA)

Boring Business Solutions (office systems company, USA)

Knot Forever (wedding planner service, India)

Peerless (urinal manufacturer, USA)

Bedwetters Irrigation Services (flower bed and lawn irrigators, USA)

Juan More Taco (taco restaurant, USA)

Boxwell Brothers (funeral directors, USA)

Dank! (bakery, Japan)

Analtech (Chemical manufacturing company, USA)

Bimbo (bakery, USA)

Nigaz (gas company, Nigeria)

Here's possibly one of the most ill-thought out names for a building company (perhaps think twice before calling on their services to deal with your erection):

STD Contractors (building contractors, USA)

Websites

Don't be fooled by this list of website addresses; they might seem ordinary at first glance, but each name contains a secret (and often foul) hidden phrase, which one can only presume the companies involved didn't intend to unleash on an unsuspecting public…

www.whorepresents.com (Who Represents)
www.expertsexchange.com (Experts Exchange)
www.penisland.net (Pen Island)
www.therapistfinder.com (Therapist Finder)
www.powergenitalia.com (Powergen Italia)
www.cummingfirst.com (First Cumming Methodist Church)
www.speedofart.com (Speed Of Art)
www.childrenswear.co.uk (Children's Wear)
www.choosespain.com (Choose Spain)
www.cumstore.co.uk (Cumbria Storage Systems Ltd)
www.dicksonweb.com (Dickson Data Ltd)
www.dollarsexchange.com (Dollars Exchange)
www.effoff.com (Effective Office Environments)
www.teacherstalk.co.uk (Teachers Talk)

www.viagrafix.net (Via Grafix)
www.wtf.org (World Taekwondo Federation)
www.nycanal.com (New York Canal)
www.ihavegas.com (IHA Vegas)
www.auctionshit.com (Auctions Hit)
www.oddsextractor.com (Odds Extractor – online betting odds)
www.redhotpawn.com (Red Hot Pawn – online chess)
www.webad.ie (Web Ad)
www.goredforwomen.org (Go Red for Women)
www.mp3shits.com (MP3s Hits)
www.newsnow.co.uk (News Now)
www.penismightier.com (Pen Is Mightier)
www.webone.com (Web One – Internet provider)

If you're planning to open a new business and want to create a website for it, perhaps it's best not to register it in the Cook Islands. See the results for yourself:

www.budget.co.ck (Budget Car Rental)
www.palm.co.ck (The Cook Islands Dive Shop)

On-screen Screamers

Some modern film titles are very literal, such as *Snakes on a Plane*. You know what to expect and you can't feel short-changed. But what about a film called *Pffft*? Could it be a profound piece about someone living with a stammer, or equally the daily life of someone who works in the Budweiser factory? Oblique titles either serve to draw you in or confuse and the same goes for video game titles – you can imagine the brains behind *Princess Tomato in Salad Kingdom* being the parent of a small child with a penchant for turkey twizzlers, trying desperately to encourage their child to eat healthily. Whatever the inspiration behind the names in this section, they are all very memorable.

Film Titles

You head into town with your friends, but it starts to rain. 'I know,' you say, 'Let's go to the cinema.' As the others shake the water from their clothes, you take the lead and buy everyone a ticket to the next film without looking at what it is – imagine your luck when you're confronted with the titles rolling up and read: *The Man Who Loved Cat Dancing.*

Here are some other titles to watch out for…

Mexican Wrestling Women vs the Aztec Mummy (1964)

The Idiot of the Mountains (1909)

Amazon Women on the Moon (1987)

Bride of the Gorilla (1951)

The Saga of the Viking Women and Their Voyage to the Waters of the Great Sea Serpent (1957)

Eegah (1962)

Don't be a Menace to South Central While Drinking Your Juice in the Hood (1996)

Hollywood Chainsaw Hookers (1988)

Phffft (1954)

Sssssss (1973)

Attack of the Killer Refrigerator (1990)

It's Dead, Let's Touch It! (1992)

Rabid Grannies (1988)

Faster, Pussycat! Kill! Kill! (1965)

This title proves that honesty isn't always the best policy when it comes to naming your future blockbuster:

Don't Worry, We'll Think of a Title (1966)

Long Film Titles

The Incredibly Strange Creatures Who Stopped Living and Became Mixed-Up Zombies (1964)

Night of the Day of the Dawn of the Son of the Bride of the Return of the Revenge of the Terror of the Attack of the Evil, Mutant, Alien, Flesh Eating, Hellbound, Zombified Living Dead Part 2: In Shocking 2-D (1991)

I Killed My Lesbian Wife, Hung Her on a Meat Hook, and Now I Have a Three-Picture Deal at Disney (1993)

Here's another (less brief) bout of cinematic honesty, with a film that does exactly what it says on the tin:

Another Demonstration of the Cliff-Guibert Fire Horse Reel, Showing a Young Girl Coming from an Office, Detaching Hose, Running with it 60 Feet, and Playing a Stream, All Inside of 30 Seconds (1900)

Video Games

Computer nerds clearly have more fun, judging by this next list of wacky nonsense…

Tongue of the Fatman

Spanky's Quest

Touch Dic (withdrawn before release and, thankfully, renamed *Touch Dictionary*)

Leisure Suit Larry 3: Passionate Patti in Pursuit of the Pulsating Pectorals

Attack of the Mutant Camels

Ninja Hamster

Ninja Baseball Bat Man

Big Mutha Truckers 2: Truck Me Harder

How to be a Complete Bastard

Tactics Ogre: Let Us Cling Together

Rex Nebular and the Cosmic Gender Bender

Princess Tomato in Salad Kingdom

Zombies Ate My Neighbours

Ninjabread Man

Wild Woody

Um Jammer Lammy

Sticky Balls

Panic Restaurant

Booby Kids

Yo! Noid

No One Can Stop Mr Domino!

And finally, included for its sheer, mind-numbing ordinariness against the thrilling action, racing and adventure games with which the market abounds:

Chemist Tycoon

Sing Along with Amputatoe

You might assume that modern-day musicians are a clean-cut bunch; slaving away in their studios to produce well-crafted records in order to please their corporate backers. You might even think that rock 'n' roll is dead. Well, not a bit of it – just take a look at some of the names in this following section and see if you still think musicians aren't as bonkers as they once were.

Song Titles

Creativity is the watchword of the music industry, but there's a fine line between creative licence and going that little bit too far. Complete disregard for the rules of music, life and occasionally even grammar characterise this next group of names…

'3/5 of a Mile in 10 Seconds' (Jefferson Airplane)

'Maybe the People Would be the Times or Between Clark and Hilldale' (Love)

'Neon Meate Dream of a Octafish' (Captain Beefheart and his Magic Band)

'Let's Face It Pal, You Didn't Need That Eye Surgery' (Don Caballero)

'Miss Mary Gets a Boob Job' (Mondo Generator)

'Windowlicker' (Aphex Twin)

'I Promise Not To Come In Your Mouth' (Frank Zappa)

'I'm a Backdoor Man' (Pauline Pantsdown)

'Bitches Ain't Shit' (Dr Dre)

'Orgasm Riddim' (Red Rat)

'A Lapdance is Always Better When the Stripper is Crying' (Bloodhound Gang)

'Short Dick Man' (Salt N' Pepa)

'When I Was a Sperm' (Master Well)

'Your Mother's Got a Penis' (Goldie Lookin' Chain)

'Judy is a Dick Slap' (Belle and Sebastian)

'My Guitar Wants to Kill Your Mama' (Frank Zappa)

'MTV Makes Me Want to Smoke Crack' (Beck)

'Detachable Penis' (King Missile)

'She Got the Goldmine (I Got the Shaft)' (Jerry Reed)

'Tequila Makes Her Clothes Fall Off' (Joe Nichols)

'She Thinks My Tractor's Sexy' (Kenny Chesney)

'Lo Boob Oscillator' (Stereolab)

'When Mama Was Moth' (Cocteau Twins)

'Franz Josef Strauss, Defence Minister, Reviews the Luftwaffe in 1958. Finding it Somewhat Lacking in Image Potential' (Robert Calvert)

'You're the Reason Our Kids Are Ugly' (Delbert McClinton)

'Everybody's Got Something to Hide Except Me and My Monkey' (The Beatles)

Now for an apparently straightforward song title which, on second reading, suddenly strikes you – how does the following situation arise? Answers on a postcard, please:

'A Lot of People Tell Me I Have a Fake British Accent' (Don Caballero)

Long Song Titles

Why use one or two words when you can use fifteen? There are plenty of incredibly long song titles; some of which take longer to say than to play the actual song...

'Several Species of Small Furry Animals Gathered Together in a Cave and Dancing with a Pict'
Pink Floyd

'Good to Know That If I Ever Need Attention All I Have to Do Is Die'
Deja Entendu

'Guy Who Got a Headache and Accidentally Saves the World'
Flaming Lips

'Like the Howling Glory of the Darkest Winds, This Voice Was Thunderous and the Words Holy, Tangling Their Way Around Our Hearts and Clutching Our Innocent Awe'
Red Sparowes

'Calling Occupants of Interplanetary Craft (The Recognised Anthem of World Contact Day)'

The Carpenters

'I Do Not Spook Easily and Those Who Think I Do Are Wasting Their Time With Surprise Attacks'

Vibracathedral Orchestra

'She Was Waitin' For Her Mother at the Station in Torino and You Know I Love You Baby But It's Getting Too Heavy to Laugh'

Shawn Philips

'We Were Stoned When We Thought Up the Title of This and We Didn't Want to Give It a Name That We Had to Explain as 'Oh Yeah We Were Stoned When We Thought of It' So We're Just Calling It Improvisational Jam 11-02-01'

!!!

'You Probably Couldn't See for the Lights But You Were Looking Straight at Me'
Arctic Monkeys

'They Provide the Paint for the Picture-Perfect Masterpiece That You Will Paint on the Inside of Your Eyelids'
Bandits of the Acoustic Revolution

'I'm a Cranky Old Yank in a Cranky Old Tank on the Streets of Yokohama with My Honolulu Mama Doin' Those Beat-o, Beat-o, Flat-on-my-seat-o Hirohito Blues'
Hoagie Carmichael

'Papyrus Containing the Spell to Preserve Its Possessor Against Attacks From He Who Is in the Water'
Nile

'Someday, in the Event that Mankind Actually Figures Out What it is That This World Revolves Around, Thousands of People are Going to be Shocked and Perplexed to Find That it is Not Them. Sometimes This Includes Me'

The Chariot

'Oh Lord, Please Bless the Rocket House and All Those Who Live Inside the Rocket House'

Forever Einstein

Whoever came up with this title was clearly in the doghouse with his missus at the time:

'You Can Make Me Dance, Sing or Anything (Even Take the Dog for a Walk, Mend a Fuse, Fold Away the Ironing Board or Any Other Domestic Shortcomings)'

The Faces

Album Titles

So, you thought those song titles were wacky? Well, imagine giving the artists concerned free scope to name their entire album. These crazy titles could blow you off your sensible little feet…

A Carrot is as Close as a Rabbit Gets to a Diamond (Captain Beefheart and his Magic Band)

The Day They Shot a Hole in the Jesus Egg – The Priest Driven Ambulance Album, Demos and Outtakes (The Flaming Lips)

The Wibbly Wobbly Walk (Anonymous)

Steal This Album (System of a Down)

I May Be Hungry But I Sure Ain't Weird (Captain Beefheart and his Magic Band)

H to He, Who Am the Only One (Van De Graaf Generator)

Locust Abortion Technician (Butthole Surfers)

Swordfishtrombones (Tom Waits)

Devin Townsend Presents Ziltoid The Omniscient (Devin Townsend)

The 5000 Spirits or the Layers of the Onion (The Incredible String Band)

Ummagumma (Pink Floyd)

Cobra and Phases Group Play Voltage in the Milky Night (Stereolab)

Everything is Alive, Everything is Breathing, Nothing is Dead and Nothing is Bleeding (The Chariot)

And finally, how about this for an album title:

When the Pawn Hits the Conflicts He Thinks Like a King What He Knows Throws the Blows When He Goes to the Fight and He'll Win the Whole Thing 'fore He Enters the Ring There's No Body to Batter When Your Mind is Your Might So When You Go Solo, You Hold Your Own Hand and Remember that Depth is the Greatest of Heights and If You Know Where You Stand, Then You Know Where to Land and If You Fall it Won't Matter, Cuz You'll Know that You're Right (Fiona Apple)

Oddly enough, it's usually known as: *When the Pawn Hits the Conflicts.*

Band Names

So, you need a name for your band. How about something like 'Dave and the Dreadnoughts' or 'The Joneses'? No? Well then, cast your eye over these bizarre monikers for some inspiration...

Holy Fuck (experimental/electronica)

Grand Master Ass-Blaster and the Pimp-Slap Crew (rock)

Hitler Stole My Potato (punk)

Boob (rock)

No Name (pop/rock)

Mr Quintron and the Flossy Unicorn Puppet Show (rock)

Paris Hitler and the Tinkerbells (punk)

Public Enema (breakbeat)

Carter the Unstoppable Sex Machine (punk)

Ed's Redeeming Qualities (alternative folk)

!!! (experimental/rock)

Toiling Midgets (post-punk)

Half Man Half Biscuit (punk)

Cod Launcher (experimental/jazz)

Thinking Fellers Union Local 282 (experimental)

Lovebucket and Slaphappy Super-Fly (rock/pop)

The Dead Milkmen (punk)

. . .And You Will Know Us By the Trail of Dead (rock)

Biffy Clyro (rock)

Porn Flakes (metal/rock)

Mussolini Headkick (industrial rock)

Amputatoe (salsa)

Gonoreagan (punk)

Cherry Poppin' Daddies (swing/ska)

Screeching Weasel (punk)

Gringo Star (rock/motown)

Iowa Beef Experience (rock)

Suburban Death Trip (rock)

Inspect Her Gadget (rock/punk)

The Al Roker Death Cult Wind Ensemble (noise/experimental)

JFKFC (dance)

Meat Beat Manifesto (electro)

Lubricated Goat (noise rock)

Circle Jerks (hardcore punk)

Avenging Lawnmowers of Justice (pop)

Fuck Buttons (experimental/progressive)

Phenobarbidols (rock)

Bearded Itchy Lover (post-psychedelic rock)

Rats Of Unusual Size (punk)

The Jackofficers (electro)

Gluecifer (hardcore rock)

Squirrel Nut Zippers (big band/jazz)

Dracula Milk Toast (grunge)

Concrete Octopus (leftfield)

A Band Named Bob (rock)

The String Cheese incident (jam band)

A Cat Born in an Oven Isn't a Cake (experimental/progressive)

Four Out of Five Doctors (pop)

Gaza Strippers (punk)

Throbbing Gristle (industrial)

Heavy Vegetable (indie rock)

Brad Pitt Live and Nude (rock)

Trotsky Icepick (post-punk)

Ear Wacks (dub)

Well Hungarians (rock)

Admiral Poopy Pants and His Dancing Teeth (rock)

Penis Flytrap (horror punk)

Ed Gein's Car (hardcore punk)

The Amazing Embarrasonic Human Karaoke Machine (rock)

Girl Scout Handgrenade (industrial)

Buddy Wasisname and the Other Fellas (ballads)

The Band Formerly Known as Sausage (rock)

Danger Wank (metal)

Jiggle the Handle (jam rock)

Planet of Pants (rock)

Gee That's a Large Beetle I Wonder If It's Poisonous (covers)

The French Are From Hell (rock)

Sorry About Your Daughter (indie)

Dick Duck and the Dorks (punk)

Bongo Sherbet and the Electrified Yeti Wobblers (rock)

IWRESTLEDABEARONCE (metal)

Thank God We're Immortal (experimental)

Global Disrobal (accoustic)

Hamster Sandwich (rock)

Turkey Makes Me Sleepy (experimental)

Spaceman Bill and the Groovy Gravy (rock)

Hindu Garage Sale (crunk)

Mustard Plug (ska)

Full Throttle Aristotle (pop)

The Sound of Animals Fighting (alternative)

Biff Hitler and the Violent Mood Swings (show music)

Exploding Head Trick (progressive)

The Insult That Made a Man Out of Mac (metal)

Jazz Iguanas (jazz)

Epileptic Disco (funk/rap)

Stop Calling Me Frank (thrash)

The Helicopter Barfs (rock)

Jolly Naked Fishermen (metal)

Man... Or Astro-Man? (surf rock)

Hot Buttered Aspirin (rock)

The Only Alternative and His Other Possibilities (pop)

Our Manager Told Us That Our Band Name Was Too Long and Difficult to Remember and That We Had to Change it So After a Long Brainstorming Session We Came Up with This One Because All the Other Ones Sucked (electronic)

Phlegm Fatale (experimental)

Rebel Without Applause (covers)

Hello I'm a Truck (rock)

Skankin' Pickle (ska punk)

Uncle Bob Touched Me (rap)

Dogs With Jobs (metal)

Zulu Leprechauns (folk/bluegrass)

When People Were Shorter and Lived by the Water (rock)

Here's a name which, at first, may not seem all that shocking – perhaps it's just an accurate description of the band as they see themselves? Well, they are certainly not from Hell; unexpectedly, the band is actually made up of Texans:

Fearless Iranians From Hell (rock)

Musical Instruments

Throughout the ages, music has continued to evolve and develop, and instruments have had to evolve too so that the progression can continue. That, however, is no excuse for naming your latest musical invention something silly – but that's exactly what the creators of these masterpieces (or otherwise) of aural pleasure have done…

Sackbut (trombone)
Crumhorn (woodwind)
Rackett (bassoon)
Serpent (woodwind)
Hurdy gurdy (fiddle)
Diddley bow (string board)
Bombard (woodwind)
Clavicytherium (harpsichord)
Orpharion (plucked string)
Banjolele (banjo/ukelele)
Sarrusophone (woodwind)
Oliphant (horn)
Heckelphone (oboe)

Theorbo (plucked string)

Crotalum (castanet)

Trautonium (electronic melody)

Ophicleide (bugle)

Viola pomposa (viola)

Now for an instrument that women everywhere would swear their husbands play whilst sleeping:

Nose whistle (whistle)

Animal, Vegetable or Mineral?

The natural world is a wonderful place, but humans always have to ruin things with silly names. I mean, who saw a beautiful, colourful snake glittering across the desert and thought, 'I know, I'll name it the *Montypythonoides riversleighensis*'? Idiot.

Animals

The following animals can probably be split into two categories: those that are so strange or unique that they need quirky names to mark them out distinctly from other, more mundane animals; and those that are so frightening that only a silly name would cheer people up when they saw one…

Chuckwalla (herbivorous desert-dwelling lizard)

Quickhatch (wolverine)

Bulbul (medium-sized passerine songbird)

Kirk's dik-dik (antelope)

Cuscus (marsupial monkey)

Spadefoot toad (toad)

Hellbender (giant salamander)

Yellow-bellied sapsucker (woodpecker)

Blobfish (deep-sea fish)

Dumbo octopus (deep-sea octopus)

Two-headed shingleback skink (omnivorous lizard)

Slender loris (small, nocturnal prosimian)

Bumblebee bat (vulnerable species of bat)

Saggy-skinned frog (frog with saggy skin, obviously)

Thorny devil (Australian lizard)

Leafy sea dragon (marine fish related to the seahorse)

Cookie-cutter shark (small, rarely-seen dogfish shark)

Blue-footed booby (long-winged sea bird)

Vampire squid (small, deep-sea cephalopod)

This fearsome-sounding creature bears no resemblance to his legendary Himalayan cousin:

The Yeti crab (blind, hairy, deep-sea crab)

Scientific Names

Here are some of the highlights from the world of animals...

Aha ha (Australian wasp)
Gammaracanthuskytodermogammarus loricatobaicalensis (amphipod)
Dolichuranus (therapsid)
Enema pan (beetle)
Ba humbugi (snail)
Indecentia (weevil)
Turbo (snail)
Cannabis (bird)
Bufonaria borisbeckeri (sea snail)
Papa (bird)
This (fly)
Vagina (clam)
Disaster (echinoid)
Batman (fish)
Troglodytes (wren)
Doryctes fartus (wasp)
Stinga (skipper)

Gammaracanthuskytodermogammarus (amphipod)
Pison eu (South American wasp)
Spartacus (leaf bug)
Atrochus (rotifer)
Eurygenius (beetle)
Chaos (protozoan)
Tubbia (fish)
Kaniwhaniwhanus (midge)
Fukuia (snail)
Scrotum humanum (dinosaur)
Gelae baen (fish)
Exetastes fornicator (wasp)
Heerz lukenatcha (braconid)
Polemistus Chewbacca (wasp)
Circus (hawk)
Darthvaderum (mite)
Silybum (thistle)
Leonardo davincii (pyralid moth)
Stupidogobius (fish)
Mamma (arachnid)
Car (weevil)
Partystona (darkling beetle)

Montypythonoides riversleighensis (snake)
Arses (monarch flycatcher)
Oops (arachnid)
Bugeranus (crane)
Pieza kake (fly)
Draculoides bramstokeri (arachnid)
Tuxedo (plant bug)
Villa sodom (bee fly)
Colon rectum (beetle)
Semen (encyrtid wasp)
Dalailama (moth from Tibet)
Boops (porgy fish)
Oxybelus cocacolae (fly-eating sand wasp)
Trivia (snail)
Verae peculya (braconid)

Whoever came up with this gem obviously felt the need to express their love of Roman history, albeit inaccurately:

Ytu brutus (water snail)

Plants

This list shows that even botanists have poetic leanings...

Aria (beam-tree)

Pinus rigida (pine tree)

Aa (orchid)

Elephantella (figwort)

Anonymos (plants)

Clitoria (butterfly-pea)

Ambrosia (ragweed)

Hallucigenia (Cambrian fossil)

Kuckuckia (brown algae)

Amorphophallus titanum (giant aroid, the world's largest flower)

This plant obviously gives everyone who sees it the willies:

Hebejeebie (alpine shrub)

Molecule Names

Individual molecules are really tiny things but they're pretty crucial in the construction of just about everything around us, so they still need names. Instead of picking something boring and ordinary, scientists have chosen more exciting monikers like moronic acid, spamol, or, in the case of one scientist who had obviously had enough of life, fucitol...

Bastardane (similar in construction to diamond, but not precious)

Megaphone (a ketone)

Cummingtonite (magnesium iron silicate hydroxide)

Dickite (a mineral similar to clay)

Moronic Acid (an acid found in some kinds of resin)

Fukalite (a type of calcium silico-carbonate)

Traumatic Acid (a plant hormone)

Fucitol (a type of alcohol)

Erotic Acid (vitamin B13)

Arsenolite (used to make glass clear)

Commic Acid (found in some kinds of plants)

Fruticolone (a ketone)

Spamol (another name for lispamol)
Diabolic Acid (a type of gas)
Gardenin (found in several types of plant)
Uranate (a variation of uranium oxide)
Welshite (named after a scientist called Welsh)
Vaginatin (found in some plants)
Antipain (a protease inhibitor)
Fornacite (a mineral containing lead)
Constipatic Acid (found in some plant life)
Penguinone (a molecule that looks like a penguin)
Apatite (a phosphate mineral)
Betweenanene (a ring-shaped molecule)

Here's a molecule that sounds like it might sneak up on you in the night and sink its microscopic fangs into your neck. Even if it really did, it would be too small for you to notice:

Draculin (found in the saliva of vampire bats)

Silly Signs

Signs are a crucial part of our lives; indeed, if we didn't have them we would all be wandering around in the hairdresser's looking for bread, or in the computer shop asking for a massage (although, if you were unlucky, you might actually find the spotty assistant agreeing to this). But this wouldn't be a book of crazy names if we hadn't scoured the earth for the wackiest shop signs around – these nutty names really are the top of the shops.

Shop Fronts

You may have noticed that some shop names seem to be trying very hard to grab your attention and entice you inside. Who cares if what they sell is any good – with names like these…

Cheeses of Nazareth (cheese shop – San Francisco, USA)
Austin Flowers (flower shop – London, UK)
Miso Hapi (Japanese restaurant – Portland, USA)
The Frying Scotsman (fish and chip shop – Paignton, UK)
O'Blivion's (Irish pub – Detroit, USA)
It's Curtains for You (curtain shop – Liverpool, UK)
Chunky Monkey (restaurant – Rhode Island, USA)
Beauty & the Beach (beauty salon – Lower Gornal, UK)
The Codfather (fish and chip shop – Isle of Wight, UK)
The Bitter End (beer shop – Tunbridge Wells, UK)
Slurp and Burp (restaurant – New York, USA)
Buy The Book (book shop – Newark-on-Trent, UK)
Battersea Cods Home (fish and chips – Sheffield, UK)
Skinny Dick's Halfway Inn (inn – Fairbanks, USA)
Paws for Thought (pet shop – Erdington, UK)
A Salt and Battery (fish and chip shop – New York, USA)

Chinee Takee Outee (Chinese takeaway – Gainsville, USA)

Thai Foon (Thai restaurant – Sydney, Australia)

Junk & Disorderly (house clearance – London, UK)

Father's Office (restaurant – Santa Monica, USA)

Squat and Gobble (restaurant – San Francisco, USA)

The Library (student bar – Tempe, USA)

Pizza the Action (pizza shop – Rugby, UK)

Aesop's Tables (restaurant – Wellfleet, USA)

Hang On (Chinese takeaway – Thatcham, UK)

The Shirley Temple (Chinese restaurant – Solihull, UK)

What Ales You (inn – Burlington, Canada)

Gobble 'n Go (restaurant – Edinburgh, UK)

The Prawnbrokers (fishmonger – Addiscombe, UK)

Dr Hogly Wogly's Tyler (Texas grill – Van Nuys, USA)

Bitter Virtue (beer shop – Southampton, UK)

Sofa So Good (sofa shop – Bury St Edmunds, UK)

Hung Far Low (Chinese restaurant – Portland, USA)

Suite Sensation (furniture shop – Birkenhead, UK)

Tan Tropez (tanning parlour – Nuneaton, UK)

Lox, Stock and Bagel (restaurant – Springfield, USA)

Air Raid Shelter (bar – Tokyo, Japan)

Road Kill Cafe (cafe – Maine, USA)
The Rock and Soul Place (fish and chips – London, UK)
Wok This Way (Thai and Cantonese takeaway – Glasgow, UK)
Three Angry Wives (Irish pub – Las Vegas, USA)
Brighton Wok (Chinese restaurant – Brighton, UK)
The Spanked Puppy (restaurant – Colchester, Canada)
Lino Ritchie (carpet shop – Finglas, Ireland)
Seoul Food (restaurant – Cambridge, USA)
Jane Armour Trading (greetings card shop – Taunton, UK)

The locals may take a sideways glance and wonder why you are having your photograph taken next to a shop or restaurant in their town, but when they have names like these, it's perfectly justified:

Farto (chemist – Sao Paulo, Brazil)
Tits (clothing shop – Montevideo, Uruguay)
Fuk Mi (sushi restaurant – location unknown)

UK Pub Names

You know you've arrived in the British countryside when you see a pub named after such things as an inebriated waterfowl or a rarely seen dromedary. Here is a list of the most bizarrely named drinking establishments…

Dirty Dicks (Bishopsgate, London)
The Three-Legged Mare (York, North Yorkshire)
The Spread Eagle (Stourhead, Wiltshire)
The Elusive Camel (Victoria, London)
The Hairy Lemon (Whitley Bay, North Yorkshire)
The Idle Cook (Idle, Bradford, Yorkshire)
Bucket of Blood (Phillack, Cornwall)
The Fawcett Inn (Portsmouth, Hampshire)
The Ram Inn (Newark, Nottinghamshire)
Moderation Inn (Reading, Berkshire)
The Pub with No Name (Priors Dean, Hampshire)
The Office (Brighton, East Sussex)
The Elbow Room (Paisley, Central Lowlands)
The Vat and Fiddle (Nottingham, Nottinghamshire)
The Happy Medium (Chichester, West Sussex)

The Hung Drawn and Quartered (Tower Hill, London)
Blooming Fuchsia (Ipswich, Suffolk)
The Cow and Snuffers (Llandaff, Cardiff)
Drunken Duck (Hawkshead, Cumbria)
The Quiet Woman (York, Yorkshire – the sign outside this pub is a woman carrying her own severed head in her hand)
Nobody Inn (Doddiscombsleigh, Devon)
The Cemetery (Rochdale, Lancashire)
The Happy Cheese (Ashurst, Hampshire)
Bung Hole (Bloomsbury, London)
The Swan With Two Necks (Little Bollington, Cheshire)
The Fourways (Delamere, Cheshire)
The Blue Ball (Sidmouth, Devon)
Rehab (Harrogate, Yorkshire)

This pub is in a more exotic region than those above (apart from Suffolk, of course). Its name conjures up grisly images of a soup that's difficult to digest but safe to swallow:

Cabbages and Condoms (Bangkok, Thailand)

Hairdressers

No industry has quite such a stranglehold on the outrageously bad pun as hairdressers – it's as though they're competing to elicit the loudest groan from passers-by. Here, we have collected some of the worst offenders, whose businesses are somehow allowed to go on styling people's hair despite their obvious lack of taste…

Hair M (Portland, Oregon, USA)

Thairapy Salon (Richmond, Virginia, USA)

Hard Az Nailz (Finsbury Park, London, UK – they also do nails, apparently)

Posh By Beck's [sic] (Hull, Yorkshire, UK)

Head Games (Portland, Maine, USA)

Lunatic Fringe (Houghton Regis, Bedfordshire, UK)

The Hair Affair (Findlay, Ohio, USA)

Go Ahead (Southgate, London, UK)

Urban Roots (Southgate, London, UK)

Hair To Stay (Villa Park, Illinois, USA)

Hairz God's Gift (Philadelphia, Pennsylvania, USA)

Julia's Scissors (Kings Heath, Birmingham, UK)

Cissors Palace (Barbican, London, UK)

The Mane Attraction (Palmer, Massachusetts, USA)
Head Bangers (Holloway, London, UK)
Hair Port (Finsbury Park, London, UK)
Upper Cut (Denver, Colorado, USA)
Mane Advocates (Manhattan, New York, USA)
Hair Hideaway (Indiana, USA)
Keep It Real (New Orleans, Louisiana, USA)
Headlites (Holloway, London, UK)
Shear Madness (Asheville, North Carolina, USA)
Hair Master (Los Angeles, California, USA)
Scissor Sisters (Chelmsford, Essex, UK)
Headmasters (Southampton, Hampshire, UK)
Curl Up and Dye (Witney, Oxfordshire, UK)
Ali Barber (Chichester, West Sussex, UK)
Chopping Block (Rhyl, Clwyd, UK)
Lobby Toffs (Sheffield, Yorkshire, UK)
Mad Hackers (Fife, Leven, UK)
Hair 2 Dye 4 (Winnipeg, Manitoba, Canada)
Hair Razor (Stafford, Staffordshire, UK)
Shear Royalty (Keokuk, Iowa, USA)
The Head Gardener (Inverness, UK)

Beachcombers (Sandhurst, Surrey, UK)
Nutters (Cambridge, Cambridgeshire, UK)
Headquarters (Kingston upon Thames, Surrey, UK)
Dye Hard (Western Springs, Illinois, USA)
Sweeney Todd's (Halifax, West Yorkshire, UK)
British Hairways (Sheffield, Yorkshire, UK)
Cliptomania (Coventry, West Midlands, UK)
Edward Scissorhands (Kinswinford, West Midlands, UK)
Debonhair (Aberdare, Mid Glamorgan, UK)
Hi De Hilites (Mitcham, London, UK)
Director's Cut (Ealing, London, UK)
Short and Curly's (Uxbridge, Middlesex, UK)
Wavelengths (Newburgh, Fife, UK)

Now for a shop where you can not only have your hair cut, but can also catch up with the latest gossip:

Short Chat and Sides (York, Yorkshire, UK)

Join the (Oddly Named) Club

It takes all sorts to make a world, and this section is dedicated to those who – perhaps somewhat surprisingly – have found enough like-minded souls to form their own club or society…

Federation Against Mind Control Europe

(Conspiracy theories abound in this protest group against state-sponsored mind control.)

Federation Against Midgets

(Rather than referring to humans, this group defines midgets as 'short ugly creatures with no nose, no ears, no knees, and… short spiky hair'.)

The UE and Mexican FAT Federation

(The translated initials stand for Authentic Workers' Front.)

The National Mullet Club

(This really refers to the common mullet, a type of fish, but the image of their AGM as one full of men and women with terrible haircuts is one of pure joy.)

The Association of Average Adjusters

(A loss-adjuster society that one can assume is populated by only mediocre types.)

The Grunt Club

(One can only imagine what goes on behind closed doors amongst the members of this group.)

Moonlight Vampire Society

(This club is clearly not for the faint-hearted – don't forget to bring some garlic.)

The Secret Society of Happy People

(A lovely thought, although it isn't so secret any more…)

The European Federation of Tall People

(This club arranges meetings between EU citizens of extreme height.)

The Idiot Club

(This is not a society for the mentally deficient, but rather the official fan club of the punk band Green Day.)

The MAD club

(Or, in full, The Midland Amateur Dancers – perhaps someone should recommend a merger with the Idiot Club…)

Now imagine yourself receiving a letter of acceptance to say you will be attending the venerable institution of higher education which goes by the name of:

Universidad de Moron

It's such a genius (excuse the dismal pun) name that it wins its own prize from this book: The Most Inappropriate Institution Name of All Time. Round of applause, please.

Mine's a Fatty Boombalatty

Anyone who enjoys the odd tipple is likely to have come across a drink of some kind with an odd or unusual name – in fact, when you're under the influence, even quite ordinary names can become quite funny. So how would you fancy supping on one or two of these beverages?

Beer

Ah, beer. A simple enough drink, you might think. So why do brewers come up with such innuendo-imbued names for their products? Is it so you have to pluck up courage just to order one? Is it solely for their own amusement? Well, whatever the reason, feast your eyes on the list below – all of these are brands you can buy around the world and all of them are as mad as a box of frogs...

... which leads us nicely into the first name on the list:

Bad Frog Beer
Santa's Butt Porter
Fatty Boombalatty
Arrogant Bastard Ale
Seriously Bad Elf
Old Leg Over
Moose Drool
Big Butt
Hell For Certain
Flying Dog in Heat Wheat
Old Leghumper
Bishop's Finger

Fiddler's Elbow

Dirty Dick's Ale

Polygamy Porter

Fat Squirrel

Stone Soup

Blithering Idiot

Old Engine Oil

Skull Splitter

Goat's Breath Bock Ale

Donkey Punch

Horse Piss

Butt Monkey Chimp Chiller Ale

This drink that might well be named after the effect it has on the drinker:

Hairy Eyeball Ale

Cocktails

Picture this: you are at a party and it's a bit boring, so you decide to liven it up by mixing up the contents of some bottles you find lying about to make a cocktail. It really is as simple as that. Well, nearly – you also have to give it the most unappetising name you can conjure up…

Sewer Rat

An Elbow in the Boobs

Horse's Ass

Good Morning to You My Love

Bitches Tit

Save the Planet

Anal Probe

Mind Your Razor

Southerly Buster

Designated Driver

Brown Cow From Hell

Tropical Fart

Freddy Fudpucker

Madam I'm Adam

Gorilla Fart

Damn the Weather

Fuzzy Navel

Income Tax

Masturbation

Rusty Nail

Bunny Hug

Cameltoe

Blood and Sand

Oh!!! Baby

Black Silk Knickers

Ernest Hemmingway Fishing Trip

Dead Chicken

Who Needs a Man?

Jamaican Banana Cooler

Imagine, having consumed a few of the above beverages, trying to ask at the bar for one of these:

Zarbooza Infatuation Investigation

It Takes All Sports

You've got to feel just a little bit sorry for sports people with funny names. You've trained for years on end, building yourself up to peak fitness with gruelling training regimes, practised for hours on end every day, spent time with coaches, psychologists and the like to make sure you're ready for the biggest race of your life, and when you cross the finish line in first place, you know your excitement will be tempered by the commentator announcing your name over the tannoy as Dick Trickle, and the resulting laughter from the crowd.

Team Names

Cheerleading must be fun – it's a healthy team activity – what's not to like? Still, it can't be any fun cheering for a team called something like Fart…

KFC Germinal Beerschot (football, Belgium)

The Providence Athletic Friars (athletics, USA)

FC KooTeePee (football, Finland)

The Elon Fighting Christians (athletics, USA)

Purdue Boilermakers (athletics, USA)

Fart (women's football, Norway)

Wichita State Shockers (baseball, USA)

The Laurel Hill Hoboes (athletics, USA)

Kampala City Council (football, Uganda)

The Gray's Harbor College of Washington Chokers (athletics, USA)

The Richmond College Thunderducks (baseball, USA)

Camel Toe (hockey, Canada)

North Carolina Tar Heels (athletics, USA)

The Deer Antlers (basketball, USA)

Deportiva Wanka (football, Peru)
The Watersmeet Nimrods (athletics, USA)

And finally, heralding from the country where ice hockey is the national sport, and revelling in a name that also sounds like a celebration of their victory on the ice:

The Macon Whoopees (ice hockey, Canada)

Sports Stars

Sports stars strive to be in a league of their own, and some are better placed than others, having been blessed with an absurd name for commentators to commit the most embarrassing faux pas – such as during the football World Cup of 1998, when commentator Brian Moore became excited as England defender Tony Adams passed the ball towards his own goalkeeper, David Seaman. What Moore uttered next is the stuff of legend: 'Adams is stretching himself, looking for Seaman.' Admittedly, it's funnier if you're a 14-year-old. Here are some other sports stars' names with plenty of chuckle potential…

Coco Crisp (baseball player, USA)

Norman Conquest (footballer, Australia)

O. J. Mayo (basketball player, USA)

Miroslav Satan (hockey player, USA)

Wonderful Terrific Monds III (baseball player, USA)

Dick Trickle (racing driver, USA)

Gaylord Perry (baseball player, USA)

Jumbo Cummings (boxer, USA)

Dick Butkus (American footballer, USA)

God Shammgod (basketball player, USA)

Urban Shocker (baseball player, USA)

World B. Free (basketball player, USA)

Argélico Fucks (footballer, Brazil)

Dick Pole (baseball player, USA)

Luscious Pusey (American footballer, USA)

Calvin Coolidge Julius Caesar Tuskahoma McLish (baseball player, USA)

Dick Seaman (racing driver, UK)

Rudy Gay (basketball player, USA)

Dikembe Mutombo Mpolondo Mukamba Jean-Jacques Wamutombo (basketball player, USA)

Ten Million (baseball player, USA)

This name is not only rude but also sounds like a particularly nasty affliction:

Rusty Kuntz (baseball player, USA)

Racehorse Names

It must be tough riding a racehorse at full gallop, hanging on by your fingertips as it vaults hedges, fences and picnicking families (if you've strayed from the track). Still, it is the commentators who need to be really skilled – in not laughing themselves hoarse at all the silly names they're reading out during the races…

Yes It's True

Braless

Watamichoppedliver

Blondeinamotel

Nosupeforyou

Short Skirt Flirt

Yes No Yes

Date More Minors

No Fat Chicks

Bodacious Ta Ta's

She Can't Say No

No Pay No Hay

Shefoggedmyglasses

Plastered

Drink Me Pretty

Sheikh'nnotstirred

Alcohol-related

Sexy Librarian

Pleasure Me

She's Well Red

Hardawn

Golden Showers

Cunning Stunt

Girls On Top

Sensible Shoes

Ménage À Trois

Strip Teaser

Rhythm Method

Jail Bait

Tit'n Your Girdle

Panty Raid

Sotally Tober

No Speed No Feed

Lags Behind

Theotherwhitemeat

She's Easy

Redhotfillypepper

Lame Jane

Chicken Lips

High Eena

Spineless Jellyfish

Hairy Potter

Thefunhasarrived

Credit Limit

Shewhomustbeobeyed

Chicks Dig Me

Reallyneededitback

Dont Choke the Cat

Reduced Sentence

Acid Reflux

Reptilian Smarts

Semi True Story

Full of Skittles

Senior Discount

Don't Buddy Me

Cerebral Concrete

Uhmm A lot

Here's a horse which could make for a very funny scene in court if its owner were to be accused of corruption:

But Your Honor

The Silliest Name Awards

Drum roll, please… it is time for the wackiest names to stand up and be counted. The winners of the Silliest Name Awards are those which display the best combination of inappropriateness, rudeness and uniqueness in their names.

Stupidity

The Mitsubishi Mum 500 Shall We Join Us

The competition was tight, and the other entrants were also very stupid, but this car name wins by a bumper. Seriously, what were they thinking?

Accidental hilarity

Cooking with Pooh

Yes, we all know that Winnie the Pooh was a character in a series of successful children's books, and that it's not the first time that a joke has been made out of it, but this really pushes the creative boundaries of accidental hilarity. It deserves to win the category by virtue of the fact that it conjures up such an unpleasant mental image.

Most inappropriate name

Lubricated Goat

They are neither lubricated nor a goat, but a rock band – a clear victory for the slippery caprines.

Most appropriate name

Kräpp

A toilet roll brand – genius!

Rudest name

Fucking

How could it have been anything else? The sign for this Austrian village has been stolen hundreds of times in the past year alone.

The funniest name

This is it – the grand prize. The most coveted award in the entire silly-name universe, chosen for its unique blend of skill and originality:

How to Pose with a Fish

The book for people who love fish a little too much! Congratulations to the creator of our magnificent winner, who wins a trip to Looneyville to celebrate with a few bottles of Old Engine Oil and some Fat Pig chocolates with their new-found friend, Nigel Bottomface. They will be travelling there in a brand new Nissan Big Thumb Harmonised Truck, and… well, you get the picture.

Know a silly name that you'd love to share with us?
Feel free to email us at: jellyfish@summersdale.com

VITAL
STATISTICS
Everything a Man Needs to Know
CHRIS WOOD

VITAL STATISTICS

Everything a Man Needs to Know

Chris Wood

ISBN: 978 1 84024 694 0 Hardback £9.99

Vital Statistics divulges the goods on sport, cars, music, films and more…

Which sporting profession has the most lucrative contracts – Formula One or Basketball?

Which pepper has the highest rating on the Scoville Scale?

What's the best-selling computer game of all time?

You'll be able to impress your mates with the answers to these questions and many more with this miscellany for the 'loaded' generation.

Test your knowledge of pubs on telly, top nightclubs, boxing weight divisions and of course football club statistics. With everything from a glossary of Japanese sex industry terms to James Bond trivia, this is the ultimate companion for the modern man.

THE WIND-UP LETTERS

From a man with too much time on his hands

Mark Hebblewhite

THE WIND-UP LETTERS

From a Man With Too Much Time on His Hands

Mark Hebblewhite

ISBN: 978 1 84024 534 9 Paperback £6.99

From a man with too much time on his hands comes this collection of barmy correspondence, guaranteed to bring a smile to even the most poker-faced customer services assistant.

Whether he's appealing to the British Lubrication Federation for advice on resolving his cat flap predicament or making an enthusiastic request to Tiffany & Co for Tiffany's autograph, Mark Hebblewhite knows how to test professional patience. If you've ever wanted to ask McVitie's whether a custard cream is really just an albino bourbon, this book has the answer – as well as the answers to some other questions you might never have thought to enquire about.

Mark Hebblewhite has been a lifeguard, a waiter and an international personal banker, as well as a vegetarian butcher and a folder of cardboard boxes in a soap powder factory. He lives on the Isle of Man.

Have you enjoyed this book? If so, why not write a review on your favourite website?

Thanks very much for buying this Summersdale book.

www.summersdale.com